Table of Contents for "Recession-Proof Your Finances: Thriving in Uncertain Times"

Introduction: Navigating Economic Uncertainty

- Understanding Recessions and Their Impact
- Why Financial Preparedness Matters

Part 1: Building a Strong Financial Foundation

- **Chapter 1: Assessing Your Current Financial Health**
    - Tracking Income, Expenses, and Debt
    - Understanding Your Financial Weaknesses
- **Chapter 2: Creating a Recession-Proof Budget**
    - Prioritizing Essential Expenses
    - Cutting Unnecessary Costs Without Sacrificing Quality of Life
    - Budgeting for Emergencies
- **Chapter 3: Eliminating Debt Strategically**
    - Identifying High-Interest Debt
    - Snowball vs. Avalanche Methods: Choosing the Right Approach
    - Negotiating with Creditors

Part 2: Growing and Protecting Your Income

- **Chapter 4: Diversifying Income Streams**
    - Exploring Side Hustles

- o Freelancing and Remote Work Opportunities
- o Passive Income Ideas That Work
- **Chapter 5: Boosting Your Career Resilience**
    - o Upskilling and Staying Relevant in the Job Market
    - o Networking for Opportunities
    - o Securing Your Current Position

Part 3: Smart Investing During a Recession

- **Chapter 6: Understanding Market Trends**
    - o What Happens to Investments During Economic Downturns
    - o Spotting Opportunities in Uncertain Times
- **Chapter 7: Safe Investments for Tough Times**
    - o Bonds, Index Funds, and Dividend Stocks
    - o Real Estate During a Recession
- **Chapter 8: Managing Risk in Your Portfolio**
    - o Diversification Strategies
    - o Knowing When to Hold, Sell, or Buy

Part 4: Planning for the Unexpected

- **Chapter 9: Building an Emergency Fund**
    - o How Much to Save and How to Get There
    - o Accessing Liquid Assets Quickly
- **Chapter 10: Securing Insurance Coverage**
    - o Types of Insurance You Need During Economic Uncertainty
    - o Avoiding Overinsurance

Part 5: Adopting a Recession-Ready Mindset

- **Chapter 11: Staying Positive Amid Financial Challenges**
    o Overcoming Stress and Anxiety About Money
    o Cultivating a Growth-Oriented Mindset
- **Chapter 12: Long-Term Financial Planning**
    o Setting Financial Goals Beyond the Recession
    o Preparing for the Next Economic Cycle

Introduction: Navigating Economic Uncertainty

Understanding Recessions and Their Impact

Recessions can feel overwhelming, as they often bring job losses, fluctuating markets, and financial insecurity. Understanding the economic forces behind recessions helps you anticipate challenges and take proactive steps to safeguard your finances. This section explains:

- What a recession is and how it affects businesses, jobs, and households.
- Common signs of an impending economic downturn.
- The emotional and financial ripple effects on individuals and families.

Why Financial Preparedness Matters

Preparation is your greatest ally during uncertain times. By creating a strong financial foundation and building resilience, you can weather economic storms with confidence. This section discusses:

- The importance of emergency funds and proactive planning.
- How financial readiness reduces stress and provides peace of mind.
- Why starting early gives you an edge in navigating economic challenges.

Part 1: Building a Strong Financial Foundation

- Chapter 1: Assessing Your Current Financial Health
  - Tracking Income, Expenses, and Debt

'Assessing Your Financial Health: Tracking Income, Debt, and Expenses'

Step 1: Understanding Your Income

Begin by gaining a clear picture of all your income sources. This includes:

- **Primary Income**: Your regular paycheck or salary.
- **Secondary Income**: Side jobs, freelance gigs, investments, or rental income.
- **Seasonal or Irregular Income**: Bonuses, commissions, or one-off earnings.

Create a comprehensive list or use tools like spreadsheets or financial apps to document your monthly and annual earnings.

Step 2: Evaluating Your Debt

Debt can be a significant obstacle during tough economic times. Understanding your debt situation involves:

- **Listing All Debts**: Include credit cards, loans, mortgages, and any other liabilities.
- **Interest Rates**: Identify which debts carry the highest interest rates to prioritize repayment.

- **Monthly Payments**: Calculate how much of your income goes toward debt repayment each month.
- **Debt-to-Income Ratio**: Determine the percentage of your income used to cover debt—ideally, this should be under 36%.

Step 3: Tracking Your Expenses

Knowing where your money goes is key to controlling your finances. To do this:

- **Categorize Expenses**: Divide into essentials (rent, utilities, groceries) and non-essentials (entertainment, dining out).
- **Analyze Spending Habits**: Identify areas where you can reduce or eliminate spending.
- **Use Tracking Tools**: Budgeting apps like Mint, YNAB (You Need A Budget), or simple spreadsheets can simplify this process.

Step 4: Summarizing Your Financial Health

After gathering all the data:

1. **Compare Income vs. Expenses**: Are you spending more than you earn?
2. **Review Savings**: How much are you setting aside for emergencies or future goals?
3. **Check Net Worth**: Subtract your total debts from your total assets to see your financial position.

'Understanding Your Financial Weaknesses'

Identifying financial weaknesses is a critical step in building a strong, recession-proof financial foundation. Here's how you can pinpoint and address areas of vulnerability in your finances:

---

1. High-Interest Debt

The Issue: Debt with high interest rates, such as credit card balances, can drain your resources and make it hard to save.
How to Identify:

- Review your debt list and prioritize those with the highest annual percentage rates (APRs).
- Calculate how much interest you're paying monthly on each account.
  How to Address:
- Focus on paying off high-interest debts first using methods like the *debt avalanche* or *debt snowball*.
- Consider consolidating or refinancing to secure lower interest rates.

---

2. Insufficient Emergency Savings

The Issue: Without a financial cushion, unexpected expenses or income disruptions can lead to financial instability.
How to Identify:

- Assess your current savings: Do you have at least 3–6 months' worth of essential living expenses?
  How to Address:

- Start small by automating monthly transfers into a dedicated savings account.
- Aim for consistent contributions, even if they're modest, to gradually build a reliable fund.

3. Overspending and Poor Budgeting

The Issue: Spending beyond your means or not tracking expenses can lead to unnecessary financial strain.
How to Identify:

- Compare your monthly expenses to your income. Are you consistently running out of funds or relying on credit?
- Look for recurring charges or subscriptions you don't actively use.
  How to Address:
- Create a realistic budget that prioritizes needs over wants.
- Use apps or spreadsheets to monitor and categorize expenses effectively.

4. Lack of Diversified Income Streams

The Issue: Relying on a single source of income increases vulnerability during economic downturns.
How to Identify:

- Review your income sources. Is your financial security tied solely to one job or business?
  How to Address:
- Explore ways to diversify, such as starting a side hustle, investing, or developing new skills to open up additional opportunities.

5. Limited Investment Knowledge or Risk Management

The Issue: Poorly diversified investments or lack of understanding about markets can lead to losses.
How to Identify:

- Assess your portfolio. Are your investments balanced and aligned with your financial goals?
  How to Address:
- Educate yourself about low-risk and recession-resistant investment options like bonds, ETFs, or dividend-paying stocks.
- Consult with a financial advisor if needed.

6. Emotional Spending or Lack of Financial Discipline

The Issue: Impulse buying or emotional spending can derail financial goals.
How to Identify:

- Review past purchases for unnecessary items bought during emotional highs or lows.
  How to Address:
- Practice mindful spending by waiting 24 hours before making non-essential purchases.
- Set clear financial goals to stay motivated and disciplined.

• Chapter 2: Creating a Recession-Proof Budget

'Prioritizing Essential Expenses'

1. Identify Essential Expenses

These are non-negotiable costs that cover your fundamental needs, such as:

- **Housing**: Rent, mortgage payments, property taxes, and homeowners/renters insurance.
- **Utilities**: Electricity, water, gas, internet, and phone bills.
- **Groceries**: Basic, nutritious food items. Prioritize home-cooked meals over dining out.
- **Transportation**: Gas, car payments, insurance, and public transport costs.
- **Healthcare**: Insurance premiums, prescription medications, and necessary medical expenses.

---

2. Categorize Spending by Priority

Rank your expenses based on their importance:

- **Must-Have (Critical)**: Housing, food, and healthcare.
- **Important (Needed but Flexible)**: Transportation and utility costs.
- **Non-Essential (Discretionary)**: Entertainment, dining out, and luxury items.

This ranking helps you allocate funds effectively, cutting back on non-essentials if needed.

3. Create a Realistic Spending Plan

- Calculate your total income and allocate at least 50% to cover essential expenses.
- Set aside 20% or more for savings and debt repayment.
- Limit discretionary spending to 30% or less.

4. Build Flexibility into Your Budget

Economic downturns are unpredictable, so prepare for potential changes:

- **Emergency Buffer**: Aim to allocate additional funds to your emergency savings, even if it means reducing discretionary spending further.
- **Adjust Monthly**: Regularly reassess your budget based on income changes or unexpected expenses.

5. Use Tools to Track Spending

- Apps like Mint, YNAB (You Need a Budget), or spreadsheets help monitor expenses and ensure you stick to your priorities.
- Automate payments for critical bills to avoid late fees and missed payments.

6. Prepare for Variable Expenses

- Include categories for occasional or seasonal costs, such as car repairs, medical emergencies, or holiday spending.
- Save proactively for these irregular expenses.

'Cutting Unnecessary Costs Without Sacrificing Quality of Life"

1. Analyze Your Spending Habits

- **Track Your Expenses**: Use apps or spreadsheets to categorize and monitor spending over 1–3 months.
- **Identify Non-Essentials**: Highlight discretionary expenses like dining out, subscriptions, or impulse buys.
- **Set Priorities**: Determine what adds real value to your life and what doesn't.

2. Optimize Essential Expenses

- **Reduce Utility Costs**:
    - Switch to energy-efficient appliances and LED bulbs.
    - Monitor heating, cooling, and water usage to lower bills.
- **Save on Groceries**:
    - Plan meals to minimize waste and shop with a list.
    - Opt for generic brands without sacrificing quality.
- **Refinance Loans**:
    - Explore options to lower interest rates on mortgages or student loans.

3. Eliminate or Downsize Non-Essential Costs

- **Cancel Unused Subscriptions**:
    - Review streaming services, gym memberships, or delivery apps.
- **Reassess Luxury Expenses**:
    - Choose fewer high-end purchases or opt for second-hand alternatives.
- **Replace Costly Habits**:
    - Make coffee at home instead of buying daily café drinks.

4. Leverage Free or Low-Cost Alternatives

- **Entertainment**:
    - Use public libraries, free streaming services, or local community events.
- **Fitness**:
    - Switch from expensive gyms to free home workouts or outdoor activities.
- **Socializing**:
    - Host potluck gatherings instead of dining out.

5. Negotiate Better Deals

- **Insurance and Utilities**:
    - Compare providers and negotiate for discounts or better rates.
- **Recurring Bills**:
    - Call service providers to inquire about loyalty programs or promotions.

6. Set Financial Boundaries

- **Implement a Spending Freeze**: Commit to a temporary halt on non-essential purchases.
- **Use Cash or Prepaid Cards**: Limit spending by using cash instead of credit cards for discretionary expenses.

7. Build Flexibility into Your Budget

- **Create a Buffer**: Set aside funds for unexpected expenses like car repairs or medical costs.
- **Reward Yourself Smartly**: Allocate a small percentage of your budget for occasional indulgences to avoid burnout.

'Budgeting for Emergencies'

Step 1: Assess Your Essential Expenses

Identify and prioritize costs that are necessary to sustain your basic needs:

- **Housing**: Rent, mortgage, utilities (electricity, water, internet).
- **Food**: Groceries and essential supplies.
- **Transportation**: Fuel, car payments, or public transport costs.
- **Insurance**: Health, auto, and home insurance premiums.
- **Healthcare**: Medications, copays, and emergency medical expenses.
- **Debt Payments**: Minimum payments on loans and credit cards.

Step 2: Eliminate Non-Essential Spending

During emergencies, discretionary spending should be reduced or paused:

- Dining out, entertainment, and luxury goods.
- Subscriptions like streaming services or gym memberships.
- Non-urgent home upgrades or travel plans.

Step 3: Create a Monthly Emergency Budget

Sum up your essential expenses and compare them to your monthly income or available savings. Allocate your resources accordingly:

- Example Breakdown:
    - **Housing**: 40%
    - **Food**: 20%
    - **Transportation**: 10%
    - **Healthcare**: 15%
    - **Debt**: 10%
    - **Miscellaneous Essentials**: 5%

Step 4: Build and Maintain an Emergency Fund

- **Savings Goal**: Aim for 3–6 months of essential expenses.
- **Start Small**: Set aside a fixed percentage of your income regularly.
- **Automate Savings**: Use automatic transfers to deposit funds into a dedicated account.

Step 5: Adjust for Income Changes

If income is reduced during an emergency:

- Reassess your budget and focus on absolute necessities.
- Look for temporary income sources, such as freelancing or part-time work.

Step 6: Use Budgeting Tools

- Utilize financial apps like Mint, YNAB (You Need A Budget), or PocketGuard to monitor spending and savings.

Step 7: Regularly Reevaluate Your Budget

- Update your budget quarterly to account for changes in expenses or income.
- Replenish your emergency fund after any significant withdrawals.

- Chapter 3: Eliminating Debt Strategically

- **Identifying High-Interest Debt**

- **Snowball vs. Avalanche Methods: Choosing the Right Approach'**

- **Negotiating with Creditors**

Identifying High-Interest Debt

The first step to effectively managing debt is to identify which obligations are costing you the most. Here's how to do it:

- **Review All Debts**: List your credit cards, personal loans, payday loans, and other obligations.
- **Compare Interest Rates**: Focus on debts with high Annual Percentage Rates (APRs).
- **Calculate the Impact**: Understand how much you're paying monthly in interest and fees to prioritize repayment.

Snowball vs. Avalanche Methods: Choosing the Right Approach

Two popular strategies for paying off debt are the snowball and avalanche methods. Selecting the right one depends on your financial situation and psychology.

- **Snowball Method**:
    - Focus on paying off the smallest debt first, regardless of interest rate.
    - Provides quick wins and boosts motivation.
    - Suitable for those who need psychological encouragement.

- **Avalanche Method**:
  - Prioritize debts with the highest interest rates.
  - Reduces overall interest paid and clears debt faster.
  - Best for those comfortable with a long-term focus.

Negotiating with Creditors

If you're struggling to manage payments, consider reaching out to creditors to negotiate better terms.

- **Lower Interest Rates**: Request a reduced APR to make payments more manageable.
- **Extended Payment Plans**: Ask for an extended term to lower monthly payments.
- **Debt Settlement**: Negotiate to settle for a lower lump-sum payment if the debt is delinquent.
- **Document Agreements**: Always get new terms or agreements in writing.

Part 2: Growing and Protecting Your Income

• Chapter 4: Diversifying Income Streams

  - Exploring Side Hustles

1. Online Job Boards and Platforms

- **General Platforms**: LinkedIn, Indeed, Glassdoor, Monster.
- **Industry-Specific**: Sites like AngelList for startups, Dribbble for creative roles, or GitHub Jobs for developers.
- **Freelance Platforms**: Upwork, Fiverr, Toptal, and Freelancer for gig and freelance work.

2. Networking

- **Professional Connections**: Leverage LinkedIn to connect with industry professionals and alumni.
- **Networking Events**: Attend industry-specific conferences or local meetups.
- **Referrals**: Ask friends or former colleagues for introductions to companies or hiring managers.

3. Direct Applications

- **Company Websites**: Check the careers page of companies you admire.
- **Cold Outreach**: Email hiring managers directly, expressing your interest and attaching your resume.

4. Staffing Agencies and Recruitment Firms

- Partner with agencies that specialize in your industry or skill set.

5. Social Media

- Use platforms like Twitter and LinkedIn to follow industry leaders and companies that post job openings.
- Join relevant Facebook or LinkedIn groups dedicated to job postings.

6. Upskilling and Certifications

- Enroll in online courses (Coursera, Udemy, edX) to acquire new skills and open opportunities in new fields.

7. Explore Emerging Trends

- Consider sectors with growing demand, such as renewable energy, healthcare tech, cybersecurity, and data analysis.

8. Volunteering or Internships

- Gain experience and build connections by offering your skills to non-profits, startups, or small businesses.

---

9. Local Community Resources

- Utilize job boards at libraries or community centers.
- Contact local chambers of commerce or workforce development organizations.

---

10. Personalized Job Alerts

- Set up alerts on job boards to receive notifications for roles that match your interests and qualifications.

- Freelancing and Remote Work Opportunities

- Passive Income Ideas That Work

Chapter 5: Boosting Your Career Resilience

- Upskilling and Staying Relevant in the Job Market

Building career resilience and staying relevant in today's ever-changing job market requires a proactive and strategic approach. Here are key strategies to upskill and ensure long-term career growth:

1. Embrace Lifelong Learning

- **Stay Updated:** Regularly read industry news, research reports, and publications to understand trends and emerging skills.
- **Enroll in Courses:** Platforms like Coursera, Udemy, and LinkedIn Learning offer courses tailored to in-demand skills.
- **Certifications:** Pursue certifications that validate your expertise, such as PMP, AWS, or Google certifications.

2. Develop a Growth Mindset

- **Adaptability:** Be open to change and embrace new challenges as opportunities to grow.
- **Feedback:** Actively seek and use constructive criticism to improve your skills.

3. Diversify Your Skill Set

- **T-Shaped Skills:** Combine deep expertise in one area with a broad understanding of related fields.

- **Soft Skills:** Hone communication, leadership, emotional intelligence, and teamwork abilities, which are valuable across industries.

4. Build Your Network

- **Professional Communities:** Join industry groups, both online (LinkedIn, Slack) and offline, to connect with like-minded professionals.
- **Mentorship:** Seek mentors who can guide you and provide career advice.
- **Networking Events:** Attend seminars, webinars, and conferences to expand your connections.

5. Leverage Technology

- **Digital Tools:** Familiarize yourself with tools and platforms relevant to your role or industry, such as project management software or AI applications.
- **Stay Tech-Savvy:** Understand the basics of AI, data analysis, and other trending technologies to remain competitive.

6. Focus on Transferable Skills

- Highlight abilities like problem-solving, adaptability, and critical thinking, which are valuable across various industries.

7. Create a Personal Brand

- **LinkedIn Presence:** Regularly update your profile and share insights to establish yourself as an industry expert.

- **Portfolio:** Showcase your skills and achievements through an online portfolio or personal website.
- **Thought Leadership:** Write articles, create content, or give talks in your area of expertise.

8. Monitor Job Market Trends

- **Industry Insights:** Use tools like Glassdoor, LinkedIn, and market reports to identify emerging roles and required skills.
- **Demand Skills:** Stay ahead by acquiring skills for roles like data analyst, cloud computing specialist, or digital marketer.

9. Seek Cross-Functional Experiences

- Take on roles or projects that expose you to different functions and departments, broadening your expertise.

10. Maintain Work-Life Balance

- Avoid burnout by prioritizing your mental and physical health, as resilience requires a well-rounded lifestyle.

- Networking for Opportunities

Identify Your Networking Goals

- **Career Growth:** Seek mentors, potential collaborators, or job opportunities.

- **Skill Development:** Connect with individuals who can teach or inspire you in new areas.
- **Visibility:** Enhance your presence in your industry or field of interest.

Utilize Various Networking Channels

- **Professional Platforms:** Use LinkedIn to connect with industry professionals and join relevant groups.
- **Conferences and Events:** Attend industry seminars, meetups, and workshops.
- **Alumni Networks:** Engage with alumni associations to leverage shared experiences.
- **Social Media:** Use platforms like Twitter, Instagram, or specialized forums to participate in discussions and showcase your expertise.

- Securing Your Current Position

1. Improve Work Performance

- **Set Clear Goals:** Understand your work objectives and consistently meet deadlines.
- **Deliver Quality Work:** Focus on details and ensure your output is of high quality.
- **Be Proactive:** Look for ways to improve processes or propose new ideas to add value to the company.

2. Build Good Relationships with Colleagues

- **Collaborate Effectively:** Work well with team members and support colleagues when needed.
- **Maintain Positive Communication:** Avoid unnecessary conflicts and stay respectful and approachable.
- **Show Reliability:** Keep your promises and fulfill your commitments.

---

3. Develop Personal Skills

- **Upgrade Technical Skills:** Stay
- **Improve Soft Skills:** Enhance communication, leadership, problem-solving, and time management abilities.
- **Continuous Learning:** Enroll in courses, attend workshops, or read professional materials regularly.

---

4. Demonstrate Flexibility and Adaptability

- **Embrace Change:** Take on new tasks or projects with a positive attitude.
- **Be Versatile:** Learn to handle multiple roles or responsibilities.
- **Crisis Management:** Stay calm and find quick, effective solutions during challenging situations.

---

5. Enhance Your Value

- **Understand Your Role:** Know how your work contributes to the company's success.

- **Show Results:** Demonstrate your value with measurable outcomes, such as increased revenue, improved efficiency, or cost savings.

6. Build Relationships with Leadership

- **Provide Updates:** Ensure leaders are aware of your contributions through regular reports or meetings.
- **Propose Ideas:** Show creativity by suggesting new solutions or initiatives.
- **Accept Feedback:** Listen to constructive criticism from management to improve your performance.

7. Protect Your Reputation

- **Be Honest:** Avoid unethical actions or behavior that violates company policies.
- **Be Thoughtful in Communication:** Refrain from engaging in negative discussions about colleagues or the company.
- **Maintain Confidentiality:** Protect sensitive information and business secrets.

8. Plan for Long-Term Growth

- **Create a Personal Development Plan:** Set clear goals for your career advancement within the company.
- **Prepare for Risks:** Have a backup plan in case the company faces challenges.

9. Increase Positive Visibility

- **Engage in Company Activities:** Show your commitment to the organization's culture by participating in events.
- **Share Achievements:** Don't hesitate to highlight your successes to management and colleagues.

10. Take Care of Your Health and Well-Being

- **Balance Work and Life:** Maintain a healthy balance to prevent burnout and stay productive.
- **Stay Positive:** A positive attitude helps you build a trustworthy and dependable image.

Part 3: Smart Investing During a Recession

Chapter 6: Understanding Market Trends

What Happens to Investments During Economic Downturns

1. Stock Market

- **Declining Valuations:** Stock prices often fall as businesses face reduced revenue, shrinking profit margins, and lower consumer spending.
- **Sector Performance:** Defensive sectors like healthcare, utilities, and consumer staples tend to perform better, while cyclical sectors such as technology, finance, and industrials often underperform.
- **Increased Volatility:** Investors react emotionally during downturns, leading to sharp fluctuations in stock prices.

---

2. Bonds

- **Government Bonds:** High-quality government bonds (e.g., U.S. Treasury bonds) are often seen as safe havens and may gain value during downturns.
- **Corporate Bonds:** Bonds from companies, especially those with lower credit ratings, may see increased default risk, leading to price declines.
- **Interest Rates Impact:** Central banks often lower interest rates to stimulate the economy, boosting bond prices but reducing yields.

3. Real Estate

- **Property Values:** Residential and commercial property values may decline due to reduced demand and higher financing costs.
- **Real Estate Investment Trusts (REITs):** Performance varies based on sector exposure; healthcare or logistics REITs may fare better than retail-focused ones.

4. Commodities

- **Falling Prices:** Demand for commodities like oil, copper, and steel often drops, causing price declines.
- **Gold as a Safe Haven:** Gold and other precious metals may retain or increase their value as investors seek stability.

5. Currency Markets

- **Safe-Haven Currencies:** The U.S. dollar, Japanese yen, and Swiss franc tend to strengthen as investors flock to stability.
- **Emerging Market Currencies:** These often depreciate due to declining investor confidence and capital outflows.

6. Alternative Investments

- **Private Equity:** Investments in startups or private companies may see slower growth or reduced valuations.
- **Hedge Funds:** The performance depends on strategy; funds focused on short-selling or market-neutral strategies may perform well.
- **Cryptocurrencies:** These can experience significant volatility, influenced by both macroeconomic factors and investor sentiment.

7. Investor Behavior

- **Risk Aversion:** Many investors shift towards safer assets, such as bonds or cash, during downturns.
- **Liquidation:** Some may sell assets to preserve capital or meet liquidity needs.
- **Long-Term Investors:** Those with diversified portfolios and a long-term view often weather the storm better.

8. Strategic Adjustments During Downturns

- **Diversify Portfolios:** Spread investments across asset classes to reduce risk.
- **Focus on Defensive Assets:** Allocate more to sectors and instruments likely to withstand economic turbulence.
- **Rebalance Regularly:** Maintain your target allocation as market fluctuations shift the balance.

- **Look for Opportunities:** Downturns often create buying opportunities for undervalued assets.

- Spotting Opportunities in Uncertain Times

1. Observe Market Shifts

- **Changing Consumer Behaviors:** Pay attention to new demands, such as increased focus on affordability or digital solutions.
- **Emerging Industries:** Look for sectors that are gaining traction due to current conditions, like renewable energy, healthcare, or technology.
- **Supply Chain Gaps:** Identify disruptions that present opportunities to provide alternative solutions.

2. Leverage Data and Analytics

- **Analyze Trends:** Use tools and reports to monitor industry changes, economic indicators, and market sentiment.
- **Identify Undervalued Assets:** Economic turmoil often creates buying opportunities in stocks, real estate, or other assets that may recover post-crisis.

3. Focus on Problem-Solving

- **Address Pain Points:** Identify the challenges people or businesses face during economic difficulties and create solutions.
- **Innovate Products or Services:** Adapt your offerings to meet current needs, such as shifting from luxury goods to essentials.

4. Keep an Eye on Government Policies

- **Stimulus Packages:** Monitor initiatives like tax breaks, grants, or subsidies that can support specific sectors or startups.
- **Regulation Changes:** New regulations or relaxations may open doors for businesses to innovate or expand.

5. Explore Alternative Revenue Streams

- **Diversify Offerings:** Introduce complementary products or services to cater to a broader audience.
- **Subscription Models:** Offer affordable, recurring payment options to retain customers during uncertain times.

6. Build Strong Relationships

- **Collaborate Strategically:** Partner with other businesses or entrepreneurs to share resources and ideas.

- **Engage with Customers:** Listen to their concerns and preferences to tailor your offerings accordingly.

7. Seek Out Distressed Assets

- **Business Acquisitions:** Struggling businesses with valuable assets or market potential may be available at lower valuations.
- **Real Estate Opportunities:** Economic downturns often lead to reduced property prices, creating investment prospects.

8. Invest in Skill Development

- **Upskill:** Enhance your capabilities in areas like digital marketing, data analytics, or finance to stay competitive.
- **Team Training:** Equip your workforce with the skills needed to adapt to new opportunities.

9. Monitor Technology and Digital Trends

- **Digital Transformation:** The shift to remote work, online education, and e-commerce opens doors for innovation in technology.
- **Automation:** Invest in tools or solutions that improve efficiency and reduce costs.

10. Stay Long-Term Focused

- **Think Beyond the Crisis:** Economic turmoil is often temporary. Investing in assets or ideas with long-term growth potential can yield significant returns.
- **Be Patient:** Opportunities may not pay off immediately but can lead to substantial gains as the economy recovers.

- ## Chapter 7: Safe Investments for Tough Times
  - Bonds, Index Funds, and Dividend Stocks

1. Bonds

Why Bonds Are Safe:

- **Fixed Income:** Bonds provide regular interest payments, making them a reliable income source during volatile times.
- **Capital Preservation:** High-quality bonds, such as government bonds, are considered low-risk and can protect your principal investment.
- **Diversification:** They typically perform well when stocks are volatile, balancing your portfolio.

Types of Bonds to Consider:

- **Government Bonds (Treasuries):** Backed by the government, these are among the safest investments.
- **Municipal Bonds:** Issued by local governments, they often offer tax advantages.
- **Corporate Bonds:** Choose high-rated corporate bonds (investment grade) for a balance of safety and returns.

Risks to Watch For:

- Inflation can erode real returns.
- Rising interest rates may reduce the market value of existing bonds.

---

2. Index Funds

Why Index Funds Are Safe:

- **Diversification:** Index funds spread your investment across a broad market, reducing the risk associated with individual stocks.
- **Low Costs:** With minimal management fees, more of your money goes into the investment itself.
- **Market Recovery Potential:** While they can decline during downturns, they tend to recover with the overall market.

Recommended Index Funds:

- **S&P 500 Index Funds:** Track the performance of the top 500 U.S. companies.
- **Bond Index Funds:** Provide broad exposure to the bond market, balancing stock market volatility.

- **International Index Funds:** Offer diversification across global markets, reducing dependence on a single economy.

Risks to Watch For:

- Market downturns can impact index funds, but staying invested for the long term often leads to recovery and growth.

---

3. Dividend Stocks

Why Dividend Stocks Are Safe:

- **Regular Income:** Dividends provide a steady cash flow, even during economic slowdowns.
- **Established Companies:** Dividend-paying companies are often well-established with stable earnings.
- **Compounding Potential:** Reinvesting dividends can accelerate portfolio growth over time.

Types of Dividend Stocks to Consider:

- **Blue-Chip Stocks:** Companies with a history of stable dividends, like Coca-Cola or Johnson & Johnson.
- **Dividend Aristocrats:** Companies that have increased dividends consistently for 25+ years.
- **Utilities and Consumer Staples:** These sectors tend to be more resilient during downturns.

Risks to Watch For:

- Dividends are not guaranteed and may be cut during severe economic crises.
- Stock prices can still decline, affecting your overall investment value.

- Real Estate During a Recession

1. Why Real Estate Can Be Safe During a Recession

- **Tangible Asset:** Real estate provides a physical, long-term investment with intrinsic value.
- **Income Potential:** Rental properties can generate consistent cash flow, even during economic slowdowns.
- **Inflation Hedge:** Real estate often retains or increases its value over time, protecting against inflation.
- **Tax Benefits:** Investors can take advantage of deductions like mortgage interest and depreciation.

2. Types of Real Estate to Consider During a Recession

Residential Real Estate

- **Single-Family Homes:** Stable demand for housing can make these properties less volatile.
- **Multifamily Properties:** Apartments and other multi-unit buildings may attract renters who are downsizing or unable to buy homes.

Commercial Real Estate

- **Essential Businesses:** Properties leased to grocery stores, pharmacies, or healthcare providers tend to perform well.
- **Industrial Real Estate:** Warehousing and logistics properties benefit from the growth of e-commerce.

REITs (Real Estate Investment Trusts)

- **Diversified Exposure:** REITs offer a way to invest in real estate without directly owning property.
- **Focus on Resilient Sectors:** Healthcare REITs, industrial REITs, and residential REITs tend to perform better during downturns.

---

3. Strategies for Investing in Real Estate During a Recession

Focus on Cash Flow

- Invest in properties with positive cash flow, where rental income exceeds expenses, to ensure a steady income stream.

Look for Distressed Properties

- Recessions often lead to foreclosures or motivated sellers, creating opportunities to buy properties at discounted prices.

Choose Stable Locations

- Invest in areas with steady demand, such as cities with diversified economies, strong job markets, or proximity to essential services.

Consider Long-Term Potential

- Hold properties through the downturn to benefit from eventual market recovery and appreciation.

4. Risks to Watch For

- **Falling Property Values:** Some real estate markets may see price declines, especially in overvalued areas.
- **Vacancies:** Economic hardship can lead to higher vacancy rates, particularly for non-essential commercial properties.
- **Financing Challenges:** Securing loans may become more difficult, or interest rates may increase for certain borrowers.

5. Tips for Managing Real Estate Investments in Tough Times

- **Build Reserves:** Maintain an emergency fund for unexpected expenses like repairs or vacancies.
- **Evaluate Tenants:** Screen tenants carefully to reduce the risk of missed rental payments.
- **Negotiate Financing:** Look for favorable mortgage terms or consider refinancing if rates drop.

- **Stay Informed:** Monitor local real estate trends and economic indicators to make informed decisions.

Case Study: Resilient Real Estate Sectors

- **Affordable Housing:** Demand often increases as individuals and families downsize to save money.
- **Healthcare Facilities:** These properties benefit from consistent demand, even during economic downturns.
- **Self-Storage Units:** Economic uncertainty can drive demand for storage as people move or downsize.

- # Chapter 8: Managing Risk in Your Portfolio

   ## - Diversification Strategies

1. Asset Class Diversification

Why It's Important

Different asset classes (e.g., stocks, bonds, real estate) respond differently to economic changes. Diversifying across these reduces overall risk.

How to Implement

- **Stocks:** Invest in various industries, company sizes (large-cap, mid-cap, small-cap), and regions (domestic and international).
- **Bonds:** Include a mix of government, corporate, and municipal bonds with varying maturities.
- **Real Estate:** Add physical properties, REITs, or real estate mutual funds for stability and inflation protection.
- **Cash or Cash Equivalents:** Maintain liquidity with assets like money market funds or treasury bills.

---

2. Sector Diversification

Why It's Important

Economic cycles affect industries differently. While one sector may decline, another might thrive.

How to Implement

- Spread investments across sectors like technology, healthcare, consumer staples, industrials, and energy.
- Allocate more to sectors expected to perform well based on current and future economic conditions.

---

3. Geographic Diversification

Why It's Important

Economic performance varies by region. Global diversification can reduce reliance on a single country's market.

How to Implement

- Invest in international stocks or mutual funds.
- Balance exposure between developed markets (e.g., U.S., Europe) and emerging markets (e.g., China, India).
- Use exchange-traded funds (ETFs) to gain broad exposure to global markets.

---

4. Investment Style Diversification

Why It's Important

Different investment styles (e.g., growth, value, income) perform differently depending on market conditions.

How to Implement

- Combine **growth stocks** (focused on capital appreciation) with **value stocks** (undervalued companies offering stability).
- Include **dividend-paying stocks** for consistent income.

5. Time Horizon Diversification

Why It's Important

Short-term and long-term investments respond differently to market volatility. Balancing these helps manage liquidity needs and growth potential.

How to Implement

- **Short-Term Investments:** Keep cash or near-cash instruments for immediate needs or opportunities.
- **Long-Term Investments:** Focus on growth-oriented assets like stocks or real estate.

6. Risk-Level Diversification

Why It's Important

Balancing high-risk and low-risk investments helps mitigate potential losses.

How to Implement

- Allocate a portion of your portfolio to conservative investments like bonds or stable blue-chip stocks.
- Invest in higher-risk assets like small-cap stocks, emerging markets, or alternative investments (e.g., cryptocurrencies) for growth potential.

7. Diversification Tools

Mutual Funds and ETFs

- These provide instant diversification by pooling resources to invest in a variety of assets or sectors.
- Examples: S&P 500 Index Fund, global bond funds, or sector-specific ETFs.

Target-Date Funds

- Adjust their allocation automatically as you approach a specific retirement or financial goal.

8. Avoid Over-Diversification

Why It's Important

Owning too many investments can dilute returns and make management complex.

How to Avoid

- Focus on meaningful diversification by selecting assets that truly reduce risk rather than duplicating exposure.
- Regularly review and rebalance your portfolio to maintain an optimal mix.

9. Rebalancing: Keeping Your Portfolio on Track

- **Why:** Over time, market fluctuations can shift your portfolio's allocation away from its intended strategy.
- **How:** Regularly sell overperforming assets and buy underperforming ones to maintain your target allocation.

10. Seek Professional Guidance

For complex portfolios or specific goals, consider working with a financial advisor. They can help design and manage a diversified portfolio tailored to your needs.

- Knowing When to Hold, Sell, or Buy

1. Knowing When to Hold

Holding investments is about maintaining your long-term strategy despite market fluctuations.

When to Hold:

- **You Have Long-Term Goals:** Investments aligned with long-term objectives should not be sold based on short-term volatility.
- **Solid Fundamentals:** The company, asset, or sector remains fundamentally strong despite temporary setbacks.
- **Dividend Income:** Stocks or funds providing steady dividends are worth holding for consistent income.
- **Market Recovery Potential:** You believe the market or specific investment will recover and grow over time.

Risk Considerations When Holding:

- Avoid emotional decisions based on fear or greed.
- Reassess periodically to ensure the asset still fits your portfolio's strategy.

---

2. Knowing When to Sell

Selling is a critical decision to lock in profits, cut losses, or rebalance your portfolio.

When to Sell:

- **Investment Goals Are Met:** The asset has achieved its target return or value.
- **Deteriorating Fundamentals:** The underlying business or asset no longer has strong financial health or growth prospects.
- **Better Opportunities:** You identify a higher-return or lower-risk investment opportunity.
- **Portfolio Imbalance:** One asset class or sector becomes overweight and increases overall risk.
- **Tax-Loss Harvesting:** Selling losing investments can offset gains and reduce your tax liability.
- **Emergency Needs:** Unexpected financial requirements may necessitate selling investments.

Avoid Selling Too Soon:

- Don't sell based on temporary market corrections or sensational news headlines.
- Review your investment thesis and confirm that the reasons for selling are logical and objective.

---

3. Knowing When to Buy

Buying involves identifying opportunities to strengthen your portfolio or take advantage of undervalued assets.

When to Buy:

- **Market Corrections:** Recessions or corrections may offer undervalued assets at discounted prices.

- **Consistent Contributions:** Regularly adding to your portfolio through dollar-cost averaging helps smooth out market volatility.
- **Positive Fundamentals:** The company, asset, or sector shows strong growth potential, stable cash flow, or other favorable metrics.
- **Diversification Needs:** Buying can help fill gaps in asset classes, industries, or geographies in your portfolio.

Risk Considerations When Buying:

- **Avoid Overpaying:** Assess valuation metrics (e.g., price-to-earnings ratios, dividend yields) to ensure the price is reasonable.
- **Understand Market Trends:** Consider the broader economic and industry-specific conditions before investing.
- **Stay Aligned With Goals:** Avoid impulsive buys and ensure the investment aligns with your risk tolerance and financial objectives.

4. Framework for Decision-Making

Regular Portfolio Reviews:

- Assess asset performance against benchmarks and your goals.
- Check for allocation drift and rebalance as needed.

Set Clear Criteria for Action:

- Define thresholds for acceptable gains or losses to trigger a buy or sell decision.
- Use tools like stop-loss orders to manage downside risk.

Monitor External Factors:

- Economic indicators, interest rates, and geopolitical events can influence when to act.

Seek Professional Advice:

If you're uncertain, a financial advisor can provide objective guidance tailored to your circumstances.

---

5. Practical Tips for Balancing Buy, Hold, and Sell Decisions

- **Stick to Your Strategy:** Avoid reacting emotionally to market noise.
- **Understand Tax Implications:** Consider capital gains taxes and holding periods when selling.
- **Diversify Gradually:** Use buying opportunities to enhance portfolio balance over time.
- **Keep Cash on Hand:** Maintain liquidity to seize buying opportunities without selling other investments at a loss.

---

6. Common Mistakes to Avoid

- **Panic Selling:** Exiting positions during market dips often leads to locking in unnecessary losses.
- **Chasing Trends:** Buying based on hype can expose you to overvalued assets or speculative bubbles.
- **Neglecting Research:** Make informed decisions rather than relying solely on past performance or advice from others.

Part 4: Planning for the Unexpected

- ## Chapter 9: Building an Emergency Fund

- How Much to Save and How to Get There

1. How Much to Save

General Rule of Thumb:

- **3–6 Months of Expenses:** Save enough to cover essential monthly expenses, such as rent/mortgage, utilities, groceries, insurance, and debt payments.
- **Adjust Based on Your Circumstances:**
    - **Single Income Households:** Aim for 6–12 months of expenses for added security.
    - **Dual Income Households:** 3–6 months may suffice since there's a backup income.
    - **Freelancers/Contractors:** Save 9–12 months of expenses due to variable income.
    - **High-Risk Careers:** If your job is in a volatile industry, consider saving on the higher end of the spectrum.

---

2. How to Calculate Your Savings Goal

1. **Determine Monthly Essential Expenses:**
    - Rent/Mortgage
    - Utilities (electricity, water, internet)
    - Groceries

- Insurance (health, car, home)
- Transportation (gas, public transport)
- Loan or credit card payments

2. **Multiply by Your Target Period:**
    - For example:
        - Monthly essentials = $2,500
        - 6 months = $2,500 × 6 = $15,000

---

3. How to Get There

Start Small, Aim Big

- **Set an Initial Goal:** Start with $1,000 as a short-term milestone, then build from there.

Budget for Savings

- **Pay Yourself First:** Treat your savings as a non-negotiable expense and automate transfers to a separate account.
- **Adjust Spending:** Cut back on non-essential expenses like dining out, subscriptions, or impulse purchases.

Increase Income Sources

- Take on side gigs or freelance work to boost earnings.
- Sell unused items online to add to your fund.

Automate Savings

- Schedule automatic transfers to a high-yield savings account or money market account.
- Allocate a percentage of your income (e.g., 10–20%) to your emergency fund.

Utilize Windfalls

- Use tax refunds, bonuses, or monetary gifts to accelerate your savings.

---

4. Where to Keep Your Emergency Fund

Safe and Accessible Options:

- **High-Yield Savings Accounts:** Offers interest growth while keeping funds liquid.
- **Money Market Accounts:** Provides slightly higher returns than regular savings accounts.
- **Certificates of Deposit (CDs):** Use for a portion of your fund if you don't anticipate needing all the money immediately.

Avoid Risky Investments:

- Do not invest your emergency fund in stocks or other volatile assets, as you may lose money or face difficulties accessing it during market downturns.

---

5. Maintaining and Growing Your Fund

- **Regular Reviews:** Reassess your fund periodically to ensure it matches your current expenses and financial goals.
- **Top-Up After Use:** If you withdraw from the fund, prioritize replenishing it as soon as possible.

6. Motivation and Tracking Progress

- **Use Visuals:** Create a progress chart or tracker to stay motivated.
- **Celebrate Milestones:** Reward yourself when you reach key savings goals.

- Accessing Liquid Assets Quickly

1. What Are Liquid Assets?

Liquid assets are those that can be quickly and easily converted into cash. These include:

- Cash in hand
- Funds in checking or savings accounts
- Money market accounts
- Certificates of deposit (CDs) with no early withdrawal penalties
- Treasury bills or short-term bonds

---

2. Best Options for Quick Access

1. High-Yield Savings Accounts (HYSA)

- **Why It's Great:** Combines liquidity with higher interest rates compared to traditional savings accounts.
- **Access Time:** Instant or same-day transfer to your primary bank account.
- **Best For:** Storing the bulk of your emergency fund while earning some interest.

2. Checking Accounts

- **Why It's Great:** Provides immediate access via ATMs, debit cards, or checks.
- **Access Time:** Instant.
- **Best For:** Keeping a portion of your emergency fund for immediate cash needs.

3. Money Market Accounts (MMA)

- **Why It's Great:** Offers check-writing and debit card access while earning interest.
- **Access Time:** Typically same day, depending on the bank.
- **Best For:** Medium-term emergencies needing quick but slightly less immediate access than checking or savings accounts.

4. No-Penalty Certificates of Deposit (CDs)

- **Why It's Great:** Allows penalty-free withdrawals, unlike traditional CDs.
- **Access Time:** May take 1–2 business days.
- **Best For:** Adding a layer of security and interest for part of your emergency fund.

5. Treasury Bills (T-Bills)

- **Why It's Great:** Highly secure, with short maturities for quick access.
- **Access Time:** Redeemable upon maturity or via the secondary market.
- **Best For:** Safe, short-term parking of a portion of your emergency fund.

6. Cash Reserves at Home

- **Why It's Great:** Provides instant access for small, immediate needs.
- **Access Time:** Instant.
- **Best For:** Emergencies like power outages or short-term cash-only needs (keep small amounts only for security reasons).

---

3. Strategies to Ensure Quick Access

Split Your Fund Strategically

- Keep a portion of your emergency fund in **immediately accessible accounts** (e.g., checking or savings).
- Allocate the rest to accounts with higher interest but slightly delayed access (e.g., HYSAs, MMAs).

Automate Transfers

- Use linked accounts to enable quick transfers between checking and savings or money market accounts.

Know Your Bank's Policies

- Be familiar with your financial institution's transfer limits, processing times, and fees for expedited transfers.

Set Up Online Banking

- Enable online or mobile banking for 24/7 access to your accounts.

Debit or ATM Card Access

- Ensure at least one portion of your emergency fund is connected to a debit or ATM card for immediate withdrawal.

---

4. Mistakes to Avoid

- **Tying Up Funds in Illiquid Investments:** Avoid placing emergency funds in stocks, mutual funds, or long-term CDs with penalties.
- **Ignoring Transfer Times:** Some accounts may take 2–3 business days for transfers; always have a faster-access option available.
- **Relying Solely on Credit:** While credit can bridge short-term gaps, it comes with interest costs and is not a replacement for an emergency fund.

---

5. Backup Options for Emergencies

If your emergency fund falls short or access is delayed:

- **Use a Low-Interest Credit Card:** As a last resort, ensure you have a card with manageable interest rates for immediate needs.
- **Tap into a Home Equity Line of Credit (HELOC):** If available, this can provide a quick borrowing option at lower rates than traditional loans.
- **Borrow from Family or Friends:** A short-term solution if you're in a bind and need immediate funds.

6. Planning for Special Scenarios

- **Natural Disasters:** Keep a small amount of cash at home for emergencies when ATMs or banks may be inaccessible.
- **Large Unexpected Costs:** Have layers in your emergency fund—some cash immediately available and more significant reserves in accounts with slightly longer access times.

- **Chapter 10: Securing Insurance Coverage**

- Types of Insurance You Need During Economic Uncertainty

1. Health Insurance

Why It's Essential:

- Medical emergencies are unpredictable and can lead to significant expenses.
- Economic downturns may result in job losses, potentially affecting employer-sponsored coverage.

What to Look For:

- Comprehensive plans covering hospital stays, prescriptions, and outpatient services.
- High-deductible health plans paired with a Health Savings Account (HSA) for cost efficiency.
- Supplemental insurance (e.g., dental, vision) if your primary plan has limited coverage.

Tips for Securing Health Insurance:

- Explore marketplace options if you lose employer-provided coverage.
- Check if you qualify for government programs like Medicaid or subsidized plans.

---

2. Life Insurance

Why It's Essential:

- Ensures financial stability for your dependents in case of your death.
- Can cover debts like mortgages, student loans, and living expenses for loved ones.

What to Look For:

- **Term Life Insurance:** Cost-effective coverage for a set period (e.g., 10–30 years).
- **Whole Life Insurance:** Combines coverage with a cash-value component for long-term planning.

Tips for Securing Life Insurance:

- Opt for term life insurance during tough economic times—it's more affordable and sufficient for most needs.
- Reassess your coverage amount based on financial obligations and dependents.

---

3. Disability Insurance

Why It's Essential:

- Replaces a portion of your income if you're unable to work due to injury or illness.
- Economic uncertainties increase stress, which can lead to health issues or workplace accidents.

What to Look For:

- **Short-Term Disability Insurance:** Covers temporary income loss (weeks to months).
- **Long-Term Disability Insurance:** Provides income replacement for extended periods, often until retirement age.

Tips for Securing Disability Insurance:

- Check if your employer offers coverage; consider supplemental policies if coverage is limited.
- Ensure the policy covers at least 60–70% of your income.

---

4. Homeowners or Renters Insurance

Why It's Essential:

- Protects your property and belongings against risks like theft, fire, or natural disasters.
- Lenders and landlords often require coverage, regardless of economic conditions.

What to Look For:

- Policies that include dwelling, liability, and personal property coverage.
- Add-ons for specific risks in your area, such as flood or earthquake insurance.

Tips for Securing Home/Renters Insurance:

- Review and update coverage to reflect the current value of your home or possessions.
- Bundle with auto insurance for potential discounts.

---

5. Auto Insurance

Why It's Essential:

- Required by law and protects against vehicle damage, theft, and liability.
- Economic stress can increase the likelihood of accidents and theft.

What to Look For:

- Minimum liability coverage as mandated by your state.
- Comprehensive and collision coverage for newer or high-value vehicles.

Tips for Securing Auto Insurance:

- Shop around for competitive rates and adjust deductibles to balance premiums with coverage.
- Maintain a clean driving record to keep premiums low.

---

6. Umbrella Insurance

Why It's Essential:

- Provides additional liability coverage beyond your standard homeowners, renters, or auto policies.
- Protects against lawsuits, which may increase during economic downturns.

What to Look For:

- Coverage limits starting at $1 million, depending on your net worth and risks.

Tips for Securing Umbrella Insurance:

- Consider if your assets or income make you a target for liability claims.
- Pair it with your existing policies for seamless coverage.

---

7. Business Insurance *(If Applicable)*

Why It's Essential:

- Protects your business against operational disruptions, liability, and property damage.
- Economic uncertainty increases risks of lawsuits and reduced income.

What to Look For:

- General liability insurance for protection against lawsuits.
- Business interruption insurance to cover lost income during disruptions.

- Cyber insurance to safeguard against data breaches and cyberattacks.

Tips for Securing Business Insurance:

- Assess your industry-specific risks and tailor coverage accordingly.
- Review policy exclusions to avoid unexpected gaps in coverage.

---

8. Unemployment Insurance

Why It's Essential:

- Provides income replacement if you lose your job during an economic downturn.

What to Look For:

- Check eligibility and benefits through your state's unemployment program.

Tips for Securing Unemployment Insurance:

- Keep your employment records and pay stubs up to date.
- Research additional assistance programs if standard unemployment benefits fall short.

- Avoiding Overinsurance

- **Evaluate Risks**: Identify the risks you face (e.g., health, property, life, business) and their potential financial impact.

- **Match Policies to Needs**: Choose policies that align with your actual exposure. For instance, if you own a modest home, there's no need for luxury-level coverage.

- **Coverage Limits**: Ensure your policy limits are appropriate for your assets, liabilities, or income.

- **Exclusions and Riders**: Avoid unnecessary add-ons or riders unless they provide specific value.

- **Cross-check Coverage**: If you already have employer-provided health insurance or travel insurance through a credit card, assess if additional standalone policies are redundant.

- **Combine Policies**: Opt for bundled policies (e.g., home and auto) to streamline coverage and avoid overlap.

- **Adjust for Life Changes**: Major life events such as buying a home, starting a family, or retirement can alter your insurance needs. Regularly review your policies to ensure they remain relevant.

- **Eliminate Outdated Policies**: Cancel coverage that is no longer needed, such as policies for old vehicles or discontinued business ventures.

Part 5: Adopting a Recession-Ready Mindset

- **Chapter 11: Staying Positive Amid Financial Challenges**

- Overcoming Stress and Anxiety About Money

- Cultivating a Growth-Oriented Mindset

Overcoming Stress and Anxiety About Money

1. **Acknowledge Your Emotions**
   - **Identify Triggers**: Recognize specific financial issues causing stress, like debt or unexpected expenses.
   - **Normalize Your Feelings**: Understand that financial anxiety is common and temporary.
2. **Take Control of Your Finances**
   - **Develop a Budget**: Track income and expenses to gain clarity. Use budgeting apps or simple spreadsheets.
   - **Address Debt Strategically**: Focus on paying high-interest debts first or explore debt consolidation options.
   - **Build an Emergency Fund**: Start small, even saving $10–$20 weekly, to create a financial buffer.
3. **Practice Stress-Relief Techniques**
   - **Mindfulness Exercises**: Meditation and deep breathing can reduce immediate stress.
   - **Physical Activity**: Regular exercise boosts mood and reduces anxiety.
   - **Creative Outlets**: Writing, art, or hobbies can help distract and relax your mind.
4. **Seek Support**

- **Professional Help**: Consult a financial advisor for guidance on debt and savings strategies.
- **Community Resources**: Leverage local programs, food banks, or housing assistance if needed.
- **Emotional Support**: Share your concerns with trusted friends or family members to lighten emotional burdens.

5. **Limit Negative Inputs**
    - Avoid unnecessary exposure to social media or news that triggers financial insecurities.

Cultivating a Growth-Oriented Mindset

1. **Reframe Challenges**
    - **View Problems as Opportunities**: Treat financial difficulties as a chance to develop resilience, discipline, and new skills.
    - **Focus on the Learning Process**: Reflect on past financial challenges and what they taught you.
2. **Set Realistic Goals**
    - **Short-Term Wins**: Set achievable, incremental goals like cutting monthly expenses by 10%.
    - **Long-Term Vision**: Envision your future financial success and plan actionable steps toward it.
3. **Embrace Change**
    - **Adaptability**: Be open to new ways of earning, saving, or investing money.

- **Continuous Learning**: Educate yourself about financial literacy through books, podcasts, or workshops.
4. **Celebrate Progress**
    - Acknowledge small successes, such as paying off a credit card or sticking to your budget for a month.
    - Use milestones to build confidence and maintain motivation.
5. **Practice Gratitude**
    - Focus on what you have rather than what you lack. Gratitude can shift your perspective and reduce stress.
6. **Surround Yourself with Positivity**
    - Connect with people who inspire and motivate you.
    - Join communities focused on growth, such as personal finance forums or self-improvement groups.
7. **Stay Solution-Oriented**
    - Instead of dwelling on problems, channel your energy into actionable solutions.

- Chapter 12: Long-Term Financial Planning

- Setting Financial Goals Beyond the Recession

1. Assess Your Current Financial Situation

- **Understand Your Net Worth**: Calculate your assets and liabilities to determine your starting point.
- **Review Spending Habits**: Identify areas where you can reduce expenses or redirect funds toward savings or investments.
- **Evaluate Debt**: Prioritize paying off high-interest debt while maintaining minimum payments on others.

2. Define Clear Financial Goals

- **Short-Term Goals (1-3 Years)**: Build an emergency fund, reduce debt, or save for a specific expense.
- **Medium-Term Goals (3-10 Years)**: Plan for milestones such as buying a home, starting a business, or funding education.
- **Long-Term Goals (10+ Years)**: Focus on retirement savings, legacy planning, or significant investments.

3. Build Resilience for Future Economic Downturns

- **Strengthen Emergency Savings**: Aim for 3–6 months' worth of living expenses in an accessible account.
- **Diversify Income Streams**: Explore side hustles, passive income sources, or investments that provide consistent returns.
- **Protect Your Assets**: Ensure you have adequate insurance coverage (health, property, life) to avoid unexpected expenses.

4. Invest with a Long-Term Perspective

- **Take Advantage of Lower Valuations**: During recessions, markets often offer opportunities for long-term investors to buy assets at a discount.
- **Focus on Diversification**: Spread investments across stocks, bonds, real estate, and other asset classes to minimize risk.
- **Contribute to Retirement Accounts**: Maximize contributions to tax-advantaged accounts like 401(k)s, IRAs, or pensions.

5. Stay Disciplined and Adaptable

- **Automate Savings and Investments**: Set up recurring transfers to ensure consistent progress toward your goals.
- **Review and Adjust Plans**: Reassess your financial strategy periodically to adapt to changes in income, expenses, or priorities.

- **Avoid Emotional Decisions**: Stay committed to your long-term plan, even during market fluctuations.

6. Invest in Yourself

- **Enhance Skills**: Use downtime during a recession to pursue education, certifications, or skill-building that increases your earning potential.
- **Expand Your Network**: Building professional connections can open doors to opportunities in both employment and entrepreneurship.

7. Plan for Legacy and Wealth Transfer

- **Create or Update a Will**: Ensure your assets are distributed according to you
- **Explore Trusts and Estate Planning**:
- **Educate Family Members**: Share financial knowledge with loved ones to promote generational financial literacy.

8. Leverage Financial Professionals

- **Financial Advisors**: Seek guidance on optimizing investments, managing risk, and planning for retirement.
- **Accountants and Tax Experts**: Use their expertise to maximize deductions, credits, and savings during tax season.

- Preparing for the Next Economic Cycle

1. Understand Economic Cycles

- **Phases of the Cycle**: Familiarize yourself with the four key phases—expansion, peak, contraction (recession), and trough.
- **Impact on Personal Finances**: Recognize how these phases affect income, employment, investments, and prices.

---

2. Build a Strong Financial Foundation

- **Emergency Fund**: Save 3–6 months' worth of expenses to cushion against job loss or unexpected costs.
- **Reduce High-Interest Debt**: Paying off credit card debt or high-interest loans reduces financial strain during downturns.
- **Create a Budget**: Maintain a clear understanding of your cash flow to make informed decisions.

---

3. Diversify Your Investments

- **Asset Allocation**: Spread investments across various asset classes (stocks, bonds, real estate) to minimize risk.

- **Rebalance Regularly**: Adjust your portfolio to align with your risk tolerance and market conditions.
- **Long-Term Perspective**: Avoid panic selling during downturns and focus on growth over time.

---

4. Strengthen Income Streams

- **Enhance Career Skills**: Continuously upgrade skills to remain competitive in the job market.
- **Develop Passive Income**: Consider rental properties, dividends, or online businesses to supplement earnings.
- **Freelancing or Side Hustles**: Build additional income sources that can sustain you if your primary income is impacted.

---

5. Plan for Inflation and Rising Costs

- **Invest in Inflation-Resilient Assets**: Consider assets like commodities, real estate, or Treasury Inflation-Protected Securities (TIPS).
- **Adjust Savings Goals**: Account for inflation in long-term savings targets like retirement or education funds.
- **Negotiate Expenses**: Lock in lower rates on loans or utilities when possible.

---

6. Stay Flexible and Adaptable

- **Maintain Liquidity**: Keep some investments in easily accessible forms, like cash or money market accounts.
- **Embrace Change**: Be ready to pivot your strategies as market conditions and personal circumstances evolve.
- **Anticipate Opportunities**: Economic downturns often create investment opportunities, such as undervalued stocks or properties.

7. Protect Your Assets

- **Insurance Coverage**: Ensure you have adequate health, property, and life insurance to mitigate unexpected losses.
- **Estate Planning**: Create or update wills and trusts to safeguard your assets for future generations.
- **Risk Management**: Consider hedging or other strategies to protect investments from volatility.

8. Stay Informed

- **Monitor Economic Indicators**: Keep an eye on unemployment rates, GDP growth, and market trends.
- **Learn Continuously**: Stay updated on financial strategies and tools through books, podcasts, or courses.
- **Seek Professional Advice**: Work with financial advisors to navigate complex decisions or market uncertainties.

9. Build a Community of Support

- **Join Financial Planning Groups**: Engage with communities that share insights and strategies.
- **Communicate with Family**: Align financial plans with loved ones to ensure mutual understanding and support.

10. Maintain a Long-Term Perspective

- **Avoid Emotional Decisions**: Economic cycles are temporary; focus on your overarching goals.
- **Celebrate Milestones**: Recognize progress toward financial independence or other benchmarks.

****

A Note of Gratitude

Dear Readers,

I would like to express my heartfelt gratitude to you for choosing this book among countless other options. Your trust and the time you've devoted to reading and experiencing this work are an incredible honor for me.

Every page, every word was written with utmost dedication and effort, in the hope that it not only delivers value but also becomes a meaningful part of your journey. Your feedback, reflections, or even just the emotions you've felt while reading are invaluable motivations that will help me improve and continue creating in the future.

Life and knowledge are unending journeys, and I hope this book has been, is, or will be a reliable companion on yours.

Once again, thank you sincerely, and I wish you all the best. I look forward to meeting you again in future works.

****

www.ingramcontent.com/pod-product-compliance
Lightning Source LLC
Chambersburg PA
CBHW071108240526
45469CB00006BD/2393